help me stop wars.
help soldiers stop wars.
help leaders stop wars.

fill me with peace and justice.
help me to work for peace and justice.
let there be peace with justice among all peoples.
—world conference of religions
for peace (wcrp)

Peace One Day

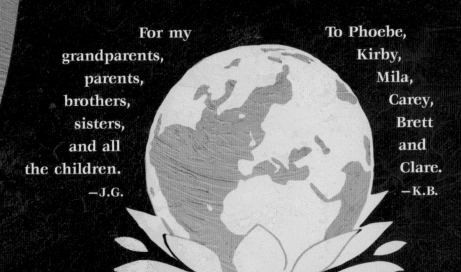

For my
grandparents,
parents,
brothers,
sisters,
and all
the children.
—J.G.

To Phoebe,
Kirby,
Mila,
Carey,
Brett
and
Clare.
—K.B.

Written by
Jeremy Gilley

Illustrated by
Karen Blessen

G. P. Putnam's Sons

The Hand Of Death

Congolese refugees head to Burundi, flee fighting

CAUTION
RADIOACTIVE

AT LEA:
25 NATIC
HAVE,
OR
MAY SO
HAVE,
NUCLEA
WEAPON

Sometimes when I'm watching TV or reading a newspaper, I think the world can be a frightening and confusing place. Innocent people lose their lives as a result of wars. People die from starvation every day.

It makes me think: *If only I could do something about it.*

But what can one person do? I remember when a rock star named Bob Geldof put on a huge concert called Live Aid to help people with no food or water. He did something. But he was famous. Could I make a difference too?

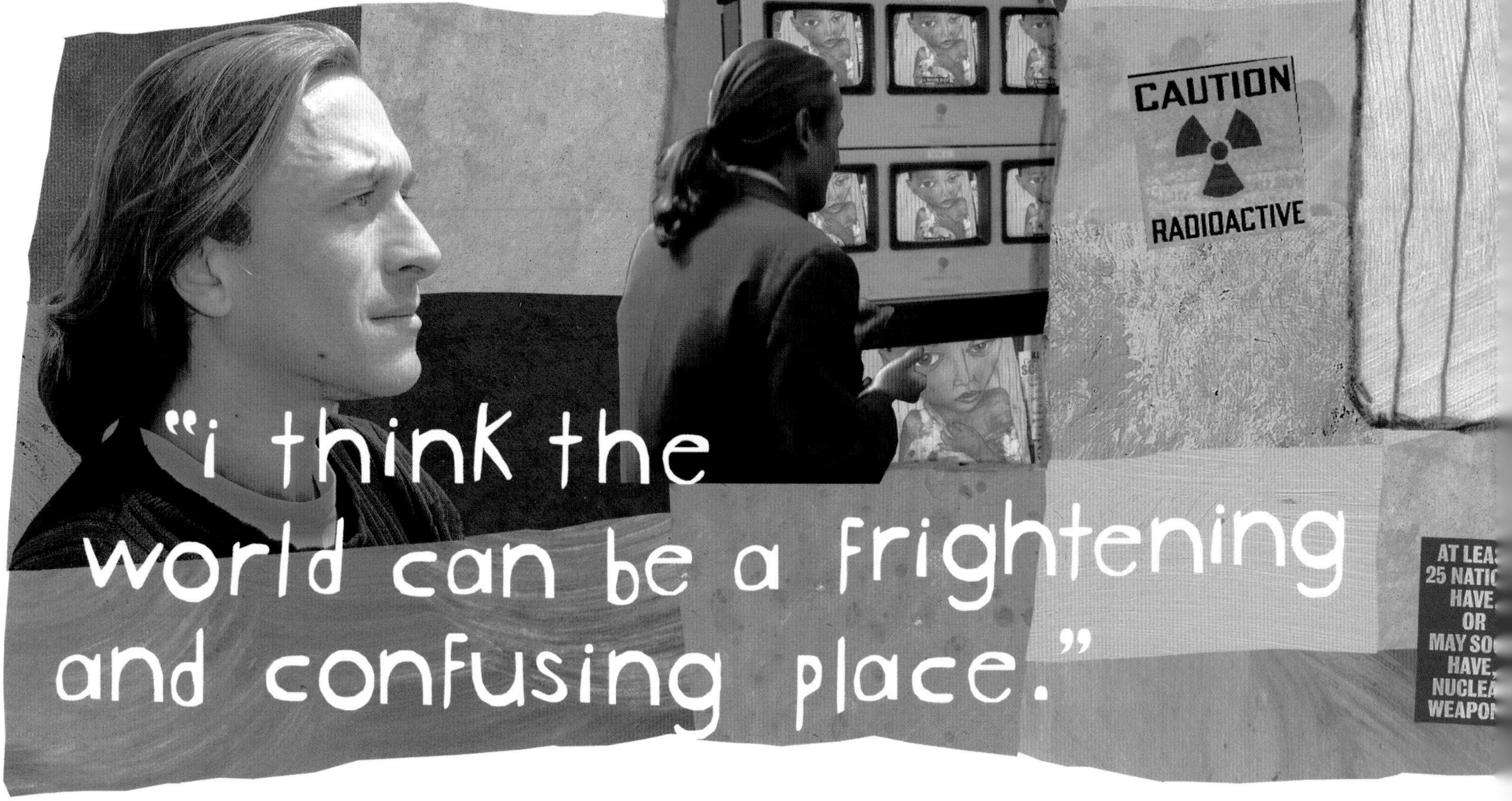

"i think the world can be a frightening and confusing place."

One day, I was at a festival celebrating music from all over the world. Everyone was dancing together and having fun. Watching all the people getting along made me wonder why the global community finds it so hard to live together peacefully. These thoughts inspired an interesting idea. What if I could create a day, like Earth Day and World AIDS Day? One day each year when all the adults and children in the world would stop fighting, a moment of unity, of intercultural cooperation. A world PEACE day, wow!

When I explained what I was going to try to do, I could tell people thought I was a little crazy! "You could never create a day of peace!" "The leaders of the world won't listen to you!" "What can one person do?"

"It won't work. why Try?"

"What can one person do?"

But these doubts just made me even more excited about trying. After all, if we only did things that we thought were possible, Thomas Edison would never have invented a lightbulb.

So where could I start?

I thought about the United Nations. Their role is to help create peace and unite the people of the world. Perhaps the UN would help me.

I wrote a letter asking if I could come and see them, to talk about my idea. They said yes. I was so excited that I forgot I didn't have any money for a flight. I called British Airways. I explained my idea and asked if they would sponsor my flights. They agreed and I nearly fell off my chair. It's amazing what you can get sometimes if you just ask. (And, by the way, it's good to say please!)

As a filmmaker, I like telling stories with my camera, so I thought while I was trying to create this day of peace, I'd film my journey so that people from all over the world could watch it and maybe learn from my experiences.

So I flew to the headquarters of the UN in New York. When I arrived, I met Sir Kieran Prendergast, Under-Secretary-General for Political Affairs. I asked him if his organization would help me create the peace day. I was very surprised when he told me there was already a United Nations International Day of Peace.

Why didn't I know about it?

United Nations BOUND

nelson mandela

mahatma gandhi

amelia earhart

mother teresa

If THERE IS TO BE PEACE IN THE WORLD, THERE MUST BE PEACE IN THE NATIONS.

IF THERE IS TO BE PEACE IN THE NATIONS, THERE MUST BE PEACE IN THE CITIES.

IF THERE IS TO BE PEACE IN THE CITIES, THERE MUST BE PEACE BETWEEN NEIGHBORS.

IF THERE IS TO BE PEACE BETWEEN NEIGHBORS, THERE MUST BE PEACE IN THE HOME.

IF THERE IS TO BE PEACE IN THE HOME, THERE MUST BE PEACE IN THE HEART.
— CHINESE PHILOSOPHER - LAO-TSE
6TH CENTURY BCE

One of the reasons the day wasn't working was because it didn't have a fixed calendar date. Each year it was supposed to fall on the third Tuesday in September, but it rarely did. It's very hard to plan in advance for a day that moves every year.

Also, the UN day of peace asked people to commemorate peace across the globe, but it didn't actually ask anyone to stop fighting.

Now I knew what I had to do!

I was going to try and set a specific date for the United Nations International Day of Peace, just like our birthdays, and also make it a day of global cease-fire and nonviolence. I chose September 21 as the date: A day for everyone in our homes, schools and communities around the world to stop fighting.

Maybe I could make a difference!

I wanted a name for the project, and after scribbling lots of ideas down, one sprung out—

PEACE ONE DAY!

I needed space to work and my mum wanted to help. She let me set up an office in her spare bedroom. My dad said he would help me account for the money I would raise and spend. For all the day-to-day work, I asked my friends to help. Whenever they could, they did.

There were lots of things I would need on my journey, and since British Airways had been so generous, I hoped other companies would be too. So whenever I needed to use a camera, sleep in a hotel or rent a car, I asked a corporation to donate their services. And they did.

SEPTEMBER 21

"Now i knew what i had to do!"

In order to change the existing United Nations International Day of Peace, I needed the support of two governments—a sponsor and a co-sponsor. They would bring a resolution to the UN General Assembly for a vote by all 189 governments.

I wrote letters to presidents, prime ministers and Nobel Peace Prize winners, asking if they would help. There were so many letters to write, envelopes to stuff and stamps to stick that I needed all the help I could get. My friends chipped in for weeks. Then I started to get replies.

One of the first people to write back was the former President of Costa Rica, Don Rodrigo Carazo Odio. The interesting thing was, he was the person who had actually created the original UN International Day of Peace back in 1981.

Soon I was flying to Central America. I had butterflies in my stomach. I'd never met a president before!

We talked about why the day hadn't been working and how a fixed calendar date would make it easier to remember and to plan lifesaving activities and celebrations. He liked my idea and told me, "If this could be done it would be a great achievement."

PAZ

"**I**F THIS COULD BE DONE IT WOULD BE A GREAT ACHIEVEMENT."

PRESIDENT DON RODRIGO CARAZO ODIO

I felt so encouraged by President Odio's words of support. What I needed now was to convince governments of the importance of creating a cease-fire and nonviolence day. So I decided to capture the real consequences of war on film.

I went to Somalia, a country in Africa where conflicts have been going on for a long time. My cameraman and I flew on a UN plane, and their security men made sure we were safe when we landed. There was no airport, just a little strip of concrete in the middle of nowhere. It was frightening, but I had to see with my own eyes what was really going on in another part of the world.

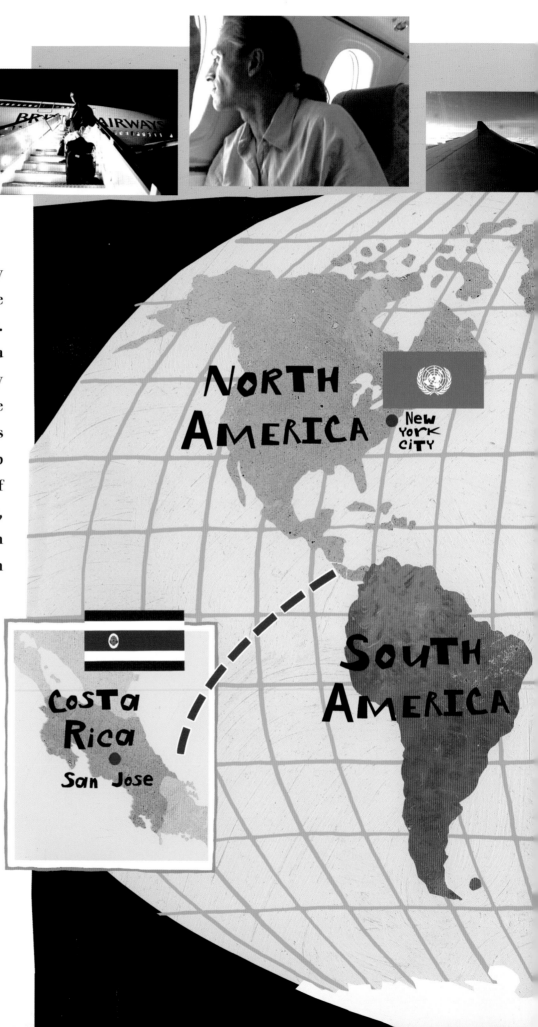

NORTH AMERICA

New YorK CiTY

CosTa Rica

San Jose

SouTH AMERICA

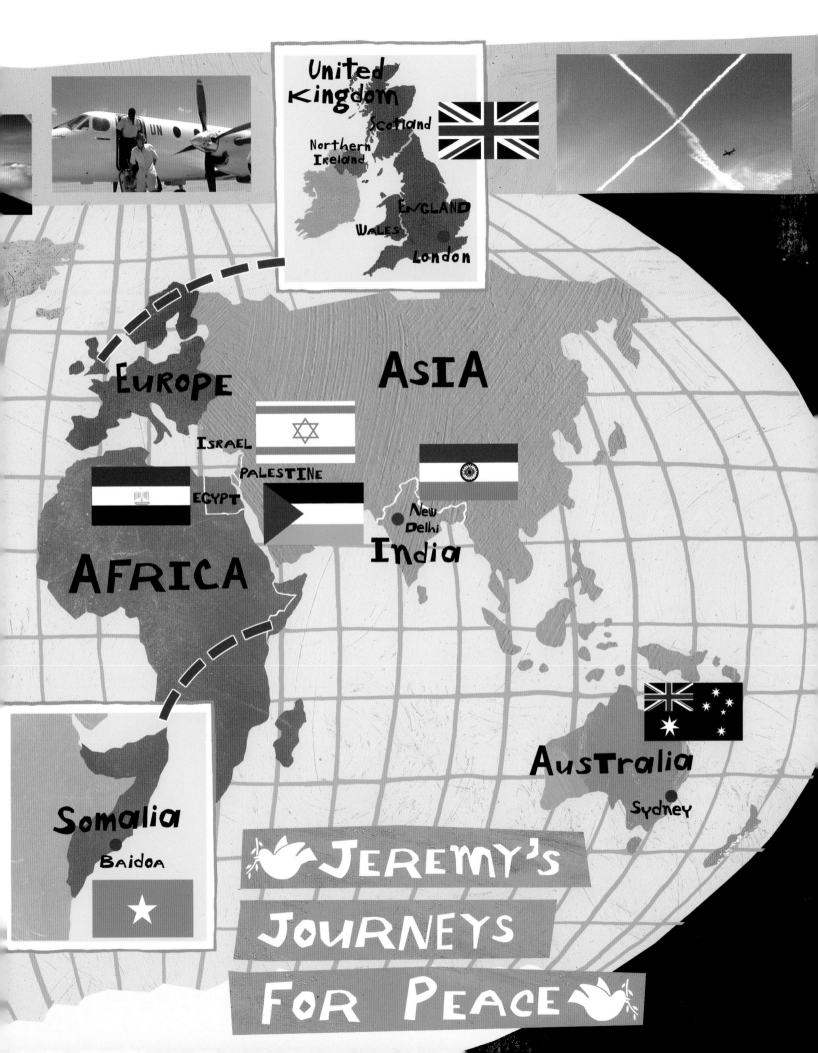

the true extent of the
devastation begins
to unfold

An estimated 300,000
children under 18
are participants in
armed conflicts in
more than thirty
countries.
— Amnesty International, 2004

What will
the world do
this time?

A night of
gunfire
that still
echoes

KIDS WITH GUNS

The town of Baidoa has always produced much of Somalia's food and clothing. Over the years, wars have been fought to control those resources. Everywhere I looked, buildings had been destroyed. Many people had to live in plastic shacks with no running water or toilets, and there was a shortage of food.

Around the world, wars over religion and land have harmed millions of children and turned many of them into fighters. So many people suffer because people won't accept differences or share the resources of our planet.

"i saw things i hope i'll never see again."

I visited an orphanage and a ten-year-old boy said, "My mother and father are dead. My three sisters and two brothers died in the war." Many children had similar stories. It was awful.

One young boy asked me a really good question. He pointed out that there are already days like African Children's Day, but they haven't changed his life at all. He said, "Don't you see that this day will be like all the other days and bring nothing positive?"

I've been asked that question many times and I always answer the same way. We've got two choices. One is to say that these days don't work and simply give up. The second choice is that we all get together and say NO, we want a global cease-fire and nonviolence day to work. It might take hundreds of years, but if we save one life in the process, it will have all been worthwhile.

Seeing the reality of war made me realize how lucky I have been to grow up without it, and I wanted even more to make a difference. The images I filmed in Somalia would make a strong case for the creation of the peace day.

"My mother, Father and sister all died From this war. This war has harmed us." —Girl, 8

I'm Afraid to Look, Afraid to Turn Away

A WORLD OF DANGER

"There is no BeneFiT...

...and we want war to stop."
—Boy, 9

it takes two countries

my friends did a lot: web master. sound technician. computer maintenance. production assistant. video coordinator. musical director. camera operator

NICARAGUA

COSTA RICA

★San Jose

PANAMA

AirMail

Jeremy Gilley
Peace One Day
London, England

Mr. Bernd Niehaus
San Jose, Costa Rica

When I got home, I wanted to tell someone from the UK government what I had learned. I hoped that the United Kingdom would be one of the countries to sponsor the resolution. I wrote a letter to Tony Brenton, Director of Global Issues for the UK Foreign and Commonwealth Office. He invited me to meet him and listened to my story. He said he would do all he could to help.

I was still hoping Costa Rica might be the other sponsor. I called Don Rodrigo Carazo Odio and asked him if he would introduce me to Mr. Bernd Niehaus, the Costa Rican Ambassador at the UN. He was the person who could put a new resolution

video editor · public relations · letter writers
travel agent · envelope stuffers · stamp sticker
telephone answerer · researcher · education coordinator

SCOTLAND

NORTHERN IRELAND

IRELAND

ENGLAND

WALES

London

UNITED KINGDOM

and a lot of friends

forward to the UN General Assembly. He agreed to a meeting, so I jumped on a plane to New York. I told Ambassador Niehaus everything that I'd learned so far about the importance of the day and why it needed a fixed calendar date. He said that it was "a beautiful idea" and was sure his government would support it.

My friends and I had to be patient and wait for these important men from the UK and Costa Rica to contact their governments. We had our fingers crossed that they would agree to put the new resolution forward!

It wasn't long before I received a very important letter inviting me to India. It was from His Holiness the Dalai Lama, Nobel Peace Prize winner and Buddhist leader. I was thrilled that this wise man had actually read my letter and taken it so seriously. The Dalai Lama is famous for encouraging nonviolence and being compassionate to others.

When I got to India, the Dalai Lama said he liked what Peace One Day was trying to do. He told me that it was up to each and every one of us to try and make a difference in the world, no matter how big or small. "We must make every effort for the promotion of peace. So I fully support," he said. I was glad he was encouraging, yet at that point I had no idea how helpful he would be in the future.

"We must make every effort for the promotion of peace."

MAY
5
2000
peace one day

His Holiness the Dalai Lama

There were other people I wanted to see in India, like the many humanitarian workers trying to help the very poor. I wondered what suggestions they might have for lifesaving activities that could take place on a day of peace.

A man from the charity Oxfam in New Delhi, the capital of India, told me if conflicts stopped even for one day, they could move food to those who were hungry. A woman from the UN children's organization UNICEF said she would be able to get medical supplies to children caught up in war. If roads were clear and people could travel without being in danger, lifesaving supplies could get through safely.

I'd learned a great deal in India. I came back with renewed enthusiasm to make the day happen. I called the Costa Rican ambassador to see if he had an answer for me yet. I couldn't get through to him on the phone, so I wrote him a letter.

What

food and water are transported.

roads are paved.

homes, buildings, and infrastructure can be fixed.

a day

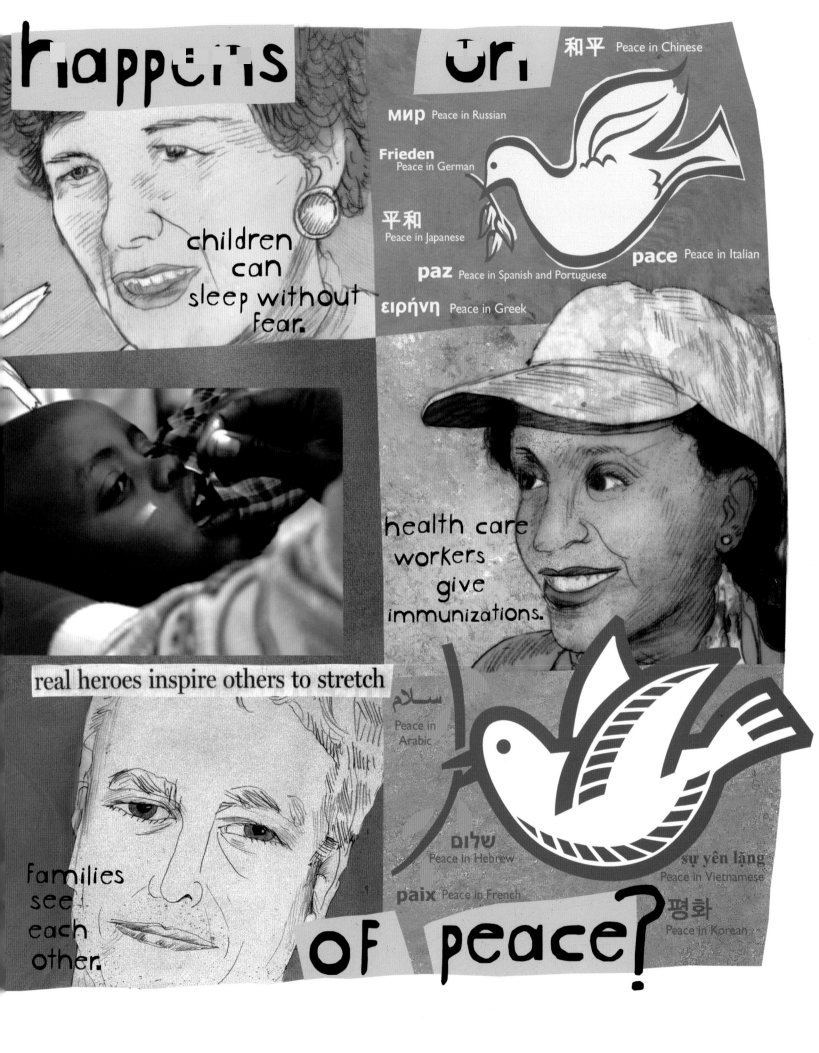

As my letter traveled west across the Atlantic, I journeyed to the Middle East.

I had been invited to Israel by Deputy Prime Minister Shimon Peres, who, along with the Palestinian leader Yasser Arafat, won the Nobel Peace Prize for trying to end the fighting between the Israeli and Palestinian people. For years I've seen pictures of people suffering in the conflict. Perhaps these two men would both agree to do what they could to end it. Perhaps they could help convince more people to observe the cease-fire and nonviolence day.

I was determined to listen and learn from both sides, but I was not prepared for the depth of emotion that was all around me. While we were filming, I had stones thrown at me. I traveled throughout Israel and Palestine, talking with families who had lost loved ones. It was very sad but at the same time somehow hopeful because the Arabs and Jews I met want peace. It surprised me that people who have lost members of their families believe in peace the most. I guess they understand how horrific it is to lose someone through war and they don't want others to experience that.

While I was in Israel, we filmed Mr. Peres saying that he fully supported Peace One Day, and he agreed if we want 365 days of peace, we need to start with the first day.

I was unable to meet with President Arafat but I did film one of his ministers, who told me, "Everyone knows it makes sense to support the idea of a global cease-fire. I take this opportunity to urge the world's youth towards peace. A movement such as this has to be the greatest in the world."

"it was very sad

My next trip was to Sydney, Australia, for the Olympics. It was almost a year since I had met with the Costa Rican and UK governments, and I was fairly sure they were about to put the resolution forward.

Throughout history the Olympics have been a time when countries come together as friends. A global event like this would be the perfect place to tell the world and the press about the creation of a world peace day.

Also, my oldest brother lives in Australia and it was wonderful to see him again. He was so supportive and helped me and my film crew find a place to stay and a car to use while we were there.

But then a crushing letter arrived. It was from the Costa Rican government, saying that they were not going to sponsor the resolution after all. I couldn't believe it. I was so upset that I felt like giving up.

"i was so upset that i felt like giving up."

I arrived home and my mom picked me up from the airport. It was great to have a big hug.

I arranged another meeting with Tony Brenton at the UK government. He said he would speak to the Costa Rican government for me and see what was wrong. I hoped he would get them back on track. I really wanted these two countries to work together and propose the resolution, but I was worried that it would all collapse. All I could do was wait.

Then something happened in my own home that made me think it was possible for people to resolve conflicts. My parents got divorced when I was three years old and their relationship wasn't great while I was growing up. But now, thirty years later, on New Year's Eve, they were dancing together as friends. It made me very happy. People can forgive in our families and they often forgive between countries. We just have to keep on believing that peace is possible.

my Family

"People can forgive in our Families

Then I got a wonderful phone call. Secretary-General of the UN Kofi Annan wanted to meet me. Wow! He was the top official at the UN. If Kofi Annan supported the idea of making the UN day of peace a global cease-fire and nonviolence day with a fixed date, that would surely help convince two governments to put the resolution forward.

For this meeting, I wanted to look very professional. I'd always liked wearing my hair long, but I wanted to fit in at the UN. It was important to be taken seriously, so my ponytail had to be chopped off!

I was very nervous about meeting Secretary-General Kofi Annan.

I was trying to remember the questions I had planned to ask him when he came in. Kofi Annan was very calm and centered. He listened to all I had to say and his response was unbelievable. He really appreciated the idea and saw lots of positive benefits. He said something that inspired me:

"I think you should continue. Individuals can make a difference and if each of us did our bit, collectively we will make a major contribution."

Hearing Kofi Annan say "I think you should continue" was the greatest encouragement I could ever receive. I was more determined than ever!

I wasn't going to give up now.

here a document

s of **Peace One Day** in

ions Global Cease-Fire

obal   awareness about such a day.

TO:

Mr. Kofi Annan, Mr. Shimon

have supported this

I have also

full support.

writing this

Chen Shui-bian,
President of Taiwan

Mary McAleese,
President of Ireland

Pope John Paul II,
Vatican, Italy

Tony Blair,
Prime Minister of UK

John Howard,
Prime Minister of Australia

Lionel Jospin,
Prime Minister of France

Silvio Berlusconi,
Prime Minister of Italy

Atal Behari Vajpayee,
Prime Minister of India

Goran Persson,
Prime Minister of Sweden

you may find

of **PEACE ONE DAY**

understand from Mr.

Peace One Day, that a

a promotional film of this project has

nt to you. With prayers and good wishes,

sincerely, **His Holiness the Dalai Lama**

On September 7, 2001, I was at the General Assembly, looking out at the representatives of all the UN countries. I watched the UK and Costa Rican ambassadors stand up and ask everyone if they would vote for the UN International Day of Peace to fall on September 21 annually, and make it a day of cease-fire and nonviolence.

There was silence.

After so much work—dozens of flights, thousands of letters, hundreds of hours given by volunteers for Peace One Day—it had come down to one moment, to one bang of a gavel.

Then the President of the General Assembly said the words I had been waiting to hear: "Do I take it the Assembly decides to adopt this resolution?"

He lifted the gavel and . . . BANG!

"It is so decided."

The world now had a true day of peace! It was the greatest day of my life. A dream come true.

I ran out of the building into the sunshine, laughing and smiling. I telephoned my family and friends. Everyone was very proud and excited.

I HAD made a difference.

"a dream come true!"

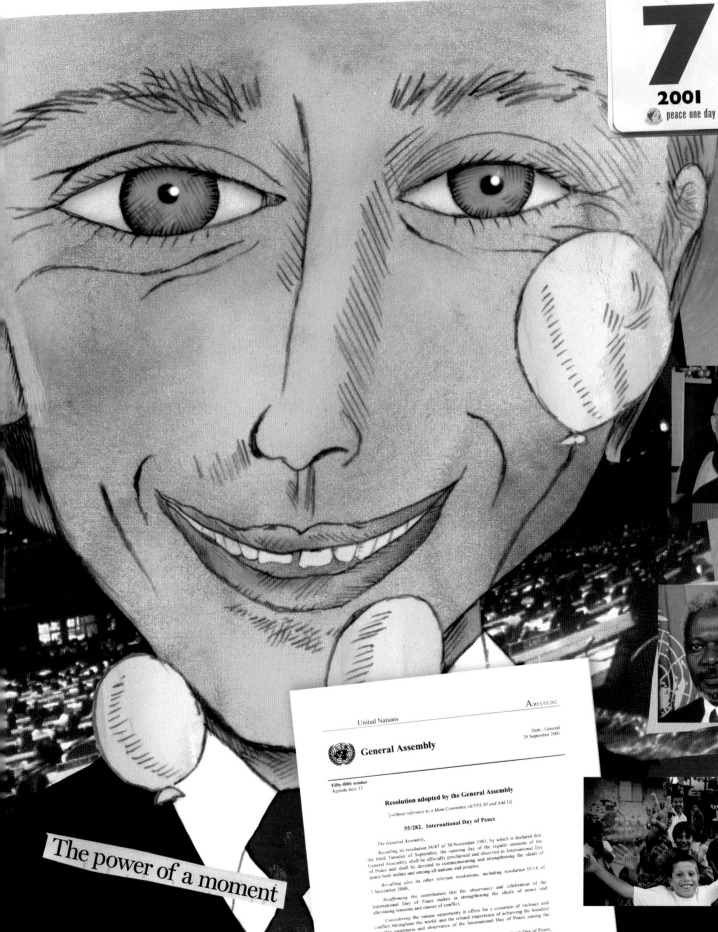

The power of a moment

A/RES/55/282

United Nations

Distr.: General
28 September 2001

General Assembly

Fifty-fifth session
Agenda item 33

Resolution adopted by the General Assembly

[without reference to a Main Committee (A/55/L.95 and Add.1)]

55/282. International Day of Peace

The General Assembly,

Recalling its resolution 36/67 of 30 November 1981, by which it declared that the third Tuesday of September, the opening day of the regular sessions of the General Assembly, shall be officially proclaimed and observed as International Day of Peace and shall be devoted to commemorating and strengthening the ideals of peace both within and among all nations and peoples,

Recalling also its other relevant resolutions, including resolution 55/14 of 1 November 2000,

Reaffirming the contribution that the observance and celebration of the International Day of Peace makes in strengthening the ideals of peace and alleviating tensions and causes of conflict,

Considering the unique opportunity it offers for a cessation of violence and conflict throughout the world, and the related importance of achieving the broadest possible awareness and observance of the International Day of Peace among the global community,

Desiring to draw attention to the objectives of the International Day of Peace, and therefore to fix a date for its observance each year that is separate from the opening day of the regular sessions of the General Assembly,

1. Decides that, with effect from the fifty-seventh session of the General Assembly, the International Day of Peace shall be observed on 21 September each year, with this date to be brought to the attention of all people for the celebration and observance of peace;

2. Declares that the International Day of Peace shall henceforth be observed as a day of global ceasefire and non-violence, an invitation to all nations and people to honour a cessation of hostilities for the duration of the Day,

"young children from different nations were playing beautiful music.

Four days later, I was invited to watch and film Secretary-General Kofi Annan at the UN headquarters. He was going to announce to the world's press that September 21, 2002, would be the first UN International Day of Peace—a day of cease-fire and nonviolence.

It was the morning of September 11, 2001. It was 8:45 A.M. and young children from different nations were playing beautiful music. And then everything changed. . . .

New York City was attacked. We were asked to evacuate the UN in case it was the next target. There was confusion everywhere. I called my mum and dad to tell them I was okay.

Tuesday, September 11, 2001

SEPTEMBER
11
2001
peace one day

Day of terror

and then everything changed."

I was worried and frightened like everyone else around me. New York City was suddenly like a war zone.

It was very strange that such a tragic event should occur on the very morning that Mr. Annan was going to announce the creation of the peace day.

The events of 9/11 demonstrated to the world the importance of a day of peace: a day for us to focus on our desire for a more peaceful world. A day of hope. A day to be empowered.

And the first one was just a year away.

"all year i looked for opportunities

I realized I had one more important job to do before my journey would be over. We had to make sure as many people as possible knew about the day so all the things we hoped would take place on a peace day could happen.

We held a press conference in London where top officials from governments, the UN and aid agencies made statements supporting the peace day. I hoped this would make the newspapers write about it, but they weren't interested.

All year I looked for opportunities to tell the world. I made a speech to a crowd at Trafalgar Square in London. I went to a soccer stadium in Germany. I went to lots of schools. My friends and I once again sent out thousands of letters asking people to make a commitment to do something for peace on the day.

I kept wondering: What would make television stations and newspapers send the message that the 21st of September was a day of peace? Then one day, someone said: "Why don't you hold a concert?" Great idea, I thought. Just like Bob Geldof. That would surely get the media interested! We began to plan and asked famous musicians to perform. They agreed.

People read about our concert in the papers. We started receiving letters, phone calls, and e-mails from people making commitments to observe the day their own way, like: "I am going to make a peace poster to hang at school." "I am going to write a letter to ask my senator to observe the day." and "I'm going to make up with my friend I've been fighting with." It was very exciting. We put all of the messages on the Peace One Day website.

We heard from people in almost 100 countries. Our friends at the United Nations were thrilled that the day was beginning to work.

Tense times,

A WORLD OF DANGER

caught in crossfire

Negotiations break down

Innocents killed

Accusations fly

Anger on the streets

Leader kill

turmoil

"i had made a **BIG** mistake!"

Just before September 21, 2002, I was invited to Cairo to meet representatives from twenty-two countries of the Arab world. I felt very honored. I wanted to make the best speech I could, to get everyone interested. If these representatives asked all the people of their countries to observe the day of peace, then surely every newspaper in the world would write about it.

I showed the short film, thinking that would get them all excited. But I was wrong. I had included an Israeli politician in the film but not a Palestinian one. This made the group very upset.

I had made a big mistake! I was reminded how delicate creating peace between two sides could be.

You know what it's like when you try and stop your friends from fighting—you have to treat both of them in the same way. I'd learned an important lesson.

There are good people from Israel and good people from Palestine and I hope one day they'll find peace.

September 21 had arrived. There were 4,500 people at the concert. It was completely full! All of my friends and family were there and everyone was jumping for joy! A lot of musicians and actors turned up to help—Jimmy Cliff, Dave Stewart, Badly Drawn Boy, Joseph Fiennes, Annie Lennox, and many others. The television cameras and newspapers recorded the night. Finally the press was telling the world.

When I stood up on stage, it was amazing! I told the audience about all the different kinds of plans that had been made in ninety-eight countries around the world.

The UN held lots of different events on the day. Secretary-General Kofi Annan rang the peace bell in New York. There were religious events where people recited a World Peace Prayer written specially for the day. Some focused on sports, like cycling for peace.

Most exciting of all, the community of Amaekpu in Nigeria used the peace day to publicly declare an end to ten years of violence and hatred. They held a celebration of unity and reconciliation to heal families and neighborhoods that had been destroyed because of fighting and civil unrest in the region.

It was beautiful. It was a fantastic start for the first September 21 world peace day.

"IT Was Beautiful.

"the community of Amaekpu in Nigeria used the peace day to publicly declare an end to ten years of violence and hatred."

SEPTEMBER
21
2002
peace one day

the concert on the
first world peace day

it was a fantastic start...

Niger

AFRICA
AREA
DETAILED

Nigeria

central
AFrican
Republic

Cameroon

atlantic
ocean

mexico

eritrea

bosnia

india

united Kingdom

norway

united Kingdom

russia

united Kingdom

united Kingdom

hong kong

united Kingdom

Kenya

nigeria

mexico

u.s.a.

mauritius

... for the first september

united kingdom

u.s.a.

SEPTEMBER
21
2002
peace one day

united kingdom

WALK FOR PEACE

u.s.a.

I can
make a
DIFFERENCE

somalia

australia

21 world peace day."

somalia

Remember what Secretary-General Kofi Annan said: "Individuals can make a difference and if each of us did our bit, collectively we will make a major contribution."

We could have a beautiful peaceful world on the 21st of September each year if everyone makes a commitment to do something. It doesn't matter how big or small, as long as you say to yourself, "It's peace day today, and one day, because of me and my commitment, our world will be united!"

When you build a house, you start with one brick. If we want to build peace, we should start with one day. And that day has arrived.

Good luck, everyone! Here's to PEACE ONE DAY!

Let's all make a difference!

peace one day

heal my wounded heart.
grant me the courage to change my heart.
let peace live in my heart.

fill me with compassion for those suffering in war.
help me care for those in war.
help me bring peace to those in war.

help me stop wars.
help soldiers stop wars.
help leaders stop wars.

fill me with peace and justice.
help me to work for peace and justice.
let there be peace with justice among all peoples.
—world conference of religions
for peace (wcrp)

september 21st

Global unity is in your hands.
Don't rely on everyone else.
What will you do on September 21st?
Make a commitment for peace at
www.peaceoneday.org.

THANKS to all the following who made Peace One Day a reality: Guy Paisner • John Battsek • Andrea Barron • Richard Wills-Cotton • Steve Barron • Damien Devine • Nick Finegold • Andrew Ruhemann • Nick Fraser • Roger Gilley • Julian Pugh-Cook • Marc Clayton • Steph Baldini • Duncan Brooker • John Bruner • Joel Doueck • Neil Elfinstone • Gagik Gharagheuzian • John Hose • Trevor Moore • David Parker • Andy Sankey • Mike Shoring • Eva Springer • Adam Tavner • Simon Chase • Caroline Coleman • Jayesh Laitha • Jack Sandham • Tam Shoring • Kelli Drinkwater • Sotira Kyriacou • Sonia Pang • Oliver Potterton • Lee Walpole • Stuart Hilliker • Boom Ltd. • Harry Escott • Matt Clarke • Kai van Beers • Darren O'Kelly • Jack Faber • Matt Williams • Andrew McKerlie • Julie-Kate Olivier • Nick Morris • Alan Cox • Fleur Easom • Leonie Gordon • Shantanu Mishra • Lewis Thorn • Tim Riding • Fay Garrett • Jenny Hyde • Jessica Ludgrove • Laura-Jayne Pearce • Naomi Glass • Christina Arfwedson • Edward Cross • Kirsty French • Emile Smith • Vicky Young • Toby Rushton • Bob Baker • Peter Richardson • Wendy Gilley • Jamie Morgan • Mark Scrancher • Edd Atcheson • Rachel Bird • Mich Ahern • Deborah Battsek • Anna Coverdale • Gaby Dior • Yael Levy • Mohamed Ayobi • Eggs Brenninkmeyer • Mikhail Ben-Shaprut • Natasa Blagojevic-Stokic • Iris Dorville • Lucile Gillmore • Paul Harris • Ahmed Hassan • Maria Esther Moro-Garcia • Helen Samuels • Mike Samra • Lionel Thomas • Massimo Marinoni • Joe Wilkinson • Eva Scrancher • Satwinder Sehmi • Fiona Spencer-Hayes • Mechthild Taylor • Jill Badolato • Zena Birch • David Blair • Charlotte Ward • Nikki Brooker • Rebekah Cairns • Rich Chaumeton • Deena Clarke • Emily Compston • Joseph Fiennes • Melisande Cook • Joanne Leonard • Rachel Cotton • Naomi Cronin • Charlie Springall • Michael Culver • Tiu De Haan • Jo Dix • Emma Robens • Gaby Douek • Kats Edwards • Sarah Fahy • Emma Fincham • Julian Flanagan • Nic Frances • Javier Garcia • Elaine Tramper • Paul Gilley • Simon Hammerstein • Suzy Harvey • Sabina Haulkhory • Davian Horlor • Samson Isaac • Kate Jackman • Nikki James • Alexandra Jerman • Salamah Khaja • Scarlet King • Nick Midgely • Christina Neville • Victoria Parker • Lili Pecirep • Isobel Pitman • Kat Popiel • Ishmael Riles • Will St. Leger • Edilaine Santos • Nadia Selatna • James Stanton • Julia Tokeley • Tora Davidson • Keisha Johnson • Darren Trute • Samantha Watt • Simon Worth • Sorrel and Amy • Lee & Thompson Solicitors • Tenon • Films Transit International • APTN • BBC • Channel 4 "RI:SE" • CNN • Granada Television Ltd. • High Spy • London News Network Ltd. • MTV • Sky • United Nations • DPI Media Division • VH1 • Ivan Mulcahy • Elisabeth Bolognini • International Olympic Committee • Roger Crago • 1 Giant Leap • Ahmad Fawzi • Damon Albarn • Kofi Annan • Badmarsh & Shri • Michael Stipe • Trevor Beattie • Richard Blackwood • Beverly Knight • Brahma Kumaris • Sir Richard Branson • Neneh Cherry • Chicken Shed Theatre Company • Coldplay • His Holiness the Dalai Lama • James DiSalvio • Omid Djalili • Faithless • Jambience • Norman Jay • Lamb • Jonny Lee Miller • Annie Lennox • Tim Bennett • Tom McRae • Moby • Mo Molam • Badly Drawn Boy • Sean Pertwee • Rhianna • Nitin Sawhney • Starsailor • Dave Stewart & Jimmy Cliff • Sugababes • Zero 7 • UNKLE • the young people of the Anna Scher Theatre • Neil McDonald • Phil Woodhead • Steve Abbiss • Mediawave • XL Video • Britannia Row Productions Ltd. • Vari*lite • Sanctuary Mobile • Music Bank • Stage Miracles • Popcorn Catering • VLPS Lighting Services • Antony Adel • Mel Agace • Len Aldis • Jim Angel • Bob Angus • Eileen Anipare • Dr. Oscar Arias • Jimmy B. • Endaye Ba • Dr. Frank Barnaby • Mary Barry • Najma Beard • Amanda Behrend • Mike Benn • Jim Benner • Brenda Bernard • Rob Bevan • Mark Boyd • Mary Brew • Marta Brnicevic • Serena Brocklebank • Sir Nigel Broomfield • Brotherhood of Saint Lawrence • Len Brown • Jess Canty • Robert Campbell • Debbie Carter • Jamie Catto • Crosby & Morag Chacksfield • Gabby Chelmicka • Joanna Clarkson • Vida Cofie-Robertson • Simon Collett • Marc Collins • Henrietta Conrad • Andy Cooper • Ken Coppel • Mairead Corrigan Maguire • Alan Cotton • Debbie Courlander • Nicky Croci • Elizabeth Crompton-Batt • Richard Curtis • Emma Diamond • Sylvia Dior • Katherine Dior • Sean Dior • Lynne Domingue • Alistair Donald • Tracy & Laurence Dunmore • Noemi Elmaleh • Scilla Elworthy • DeNica Fairman • Keith Field • Rebecca Fiest • Veronique Foucault • Nic Frances • Morissa Franks • Mike Fraser • Malec Fustok • Shaina Galvin • Jimmy Gardner • Jeremy Gawade • Ant Genn • Malcolm Gerrie • Jeremy Gibson • Lord David Gillmore • Steve Glick • Richard Godfrey • Molly Grad • Peter Greensmith • John Guinness • Sabrina Guinness • Dena Hammerstein • Nick Hanks • Eirwen Harbottle • Juliet Harris • Paul & Sam Harris • Toby Hartwell • Adrian Henriques • Merlin Patrick-Hogarth • Luke Hyams • David Irving • Carolyn Jackson • Michael Jacobs • Richard Jacobs • Dadi Janki • Tim Jobling • Jojo & Tunde • Pat Joseph • The Rt. Hon. Gerald Kaufman M.P. • Tiggy Kennedy Tony Kent • Duncan Kenworthy • Brian Kercher • Ian King • Gillian Kitching • Daniel & Judy Kleinman • Kevin Kollenda • Mark Koops • Fred Kwafo • Ben Lacy • Ladas & Parry • Mark Lambert • Shirley Lavis • Sigi Leigh • Mike Lubin • Niall MacAnna • Stella McCartney • Jackie McQuillan • James Meers • Todd and Lauren Merrill • Michael Michalski • Sean Millar • Sir John Mills • Helen Mirren • Lady Fiona Montagu • Sara Novakovic • Michael Nyman • Dan Oakes • Mark O'Sullivan • Deepa Parbhoo • Imogen Parsons • Oliver Peyton • Michael Philipp • Trent Philipp • Lena Pietsch • David Pinder • Penni Pike • Joan Plowright CBE • Robert Posner • David Pounds • Sir Kieran Prendergast • Tara Preston • Maggie Prosser • Jo Ralling • Terri Razell • Caroline Reason • Penny Richards • Alan Rickman • Wob Roberts • John Royan • Sofia Rychlik-Hadley • Mark Rylance • Sir Sydney Samuelson • John Sands • Anna Scher • Nicholas Schofield • Mark Schwartz • Karen See • Fazal Shah • Steven Shailer • Sharn Sharma • Caroline Sharp • Fiona Shaw • Michael Sherwood • Matthew Showering • Ben Silverman • Carolyn Smith • Mary Smyth • Tracy Standish • Caroline Stirling • Lee Stone • Georgie Summerhayes • Christopher Sylvester • Maryam Taheri • Matt Taylor • Sam Taylor-Wood • Shashi Tharoor • Teun Timmers • Nick Turnbull • Dan Wagner • David Walker • Liza Walker • Simon Walker • Mark Westbrook • Isabel Williams • Nigel Woodford • Clive Wright • Gill Wright • Neil Wyatt • Carmen Zita • adidas • Air Lanka • Artist Independent Network • Artist Network Ltd. • Avid Technology Europe Ltd. • Bowlplex • British Airways • Productions Ltd. • Camera Service Center Inc. • Chinagraph • Colors Magazine • Colour Film Services • Central Hire • Cropmarks • Direct Connection • Diverse Ltd. • Dubbs • Data Gate • ECB PR • El Al Israel Airlines • Europcar • Execution Ltd. • Firebrand • Forte Hotel Group • HHB Communications • Host 365 • Hyperactive Publicity • High Spy • Ice Film • I.E. Music • Image Bank • International Management Group • Jet Airways • Joe's Basement • Kodak • McMillan UK Ltd. • Metro • Metropolis Music • Microsoft • The Mill • MSN • Netscalibur UK Ltd. • Nice Shoes • Olivers Health Food Shop • Panavision • Passion Pictures • Paul Weiland Productions • PioneeringSpirit • Prime TV • Real Networks • Richmond Film Services • Samfreight • Shakespeare's Globe Theatre, London • Sony • Swim Productions • Taj Hotel Group • TBWA • THB Media • The Picture Canning Company • Translux • Trans World International • Venda • Video Europe • Virgin • Vodafone • Warwick Sound • Webactive • Westbrook Hair • William Morris • Woodhead Caliva • The Yard • BMG Music Publishing Ltd., Champion Music Ltd. • BMG UK & Ireland Ltd. • Invasion Group Ltd. • Mark Rutherford • Santana • EMI Music Publishing Ltd. • Arista Records, Inc. • Lenny Kravitz • Inc./Virgin Records Ltd. • Samir Khanjar • Drew Galligan • Karen Blessen • David Friend • Nancy Paulsen • Susan Kochan • Cindy Howle • Cecilia Yung • Gunta Alexander • Sara Kreger • L. Subramaniam • Niranjani Music Co. • Erato Disques S.A. • Warner Chappell Music Ltd. • Palm Pictures Ltd. • Les Jumeaux • Chicane • Universal/MCA Music Ltd. • Warner Strategic Marketing UK • Ryuichi Sakamoto • Kab America Inc. • Royal Liverpool Philharmonic • Hoyt Axton • Samuel Barber • MC Sultan • Edition Spray • The Orchestra of The Royal Opera House • Bob Marley • Fifty-Six Hope Road Music Ltd. • Odnil Music Ltd. • Blue Mountain Music Ltd. • Fairwood Music Ltd. • Universal-Island Records Ltd. • Johnny Nash. • Thank you to Nancy and David for believing. —J. G.

THANK YOU to Nancy Paulsen, Susan Kochan, and Cecilia Yung at Putnam for the opportunity to do this book! Thank you to designer Gunta Alexander for making it all come together. A special thank-you to my agents, Vicki Morgan and Gail Gaynin at Morgan Gaynin. Love you! Thanks to Angi Brown, Ginny Martin, Oksana Kiryanova and Bette Buschow for your expertise and assistance. Thank you to my artist friends Lamberto Alvarez, Marilyn Bishkin, and Julie Cohn for giving me your eyes and guidance. A special thanks to Gretchen Dykstra for being a friend and catalyst. For the usage of extraordinary photographs, thank you to the photography department of *The Dallas Morning News* and to Gulnara Samoilova.

And finally, two extra special thank-yous. First, to Jeremy Gilley, for the humbling opportunity to collaborate and extend the hope of peace in our world, and to visually tell your story of perseverance and vision. Lastly, a big thank-you and smile to my sweet husband, Kelly Nash, who knows just the moment to say: "Everything's going to be great!" —K. B.

Photographic images supplied by Peace One Day © 2005 by Peace One Day Limited. THANKS to the following photographers who collected images for Peace One Day: Lighting Camera: Ole Bratt Birkeland - Chester Dent - Chris Diaper - Mary Farbrother - Paul Gillmore - Jim Jolliffe - Alvin Leong - Martin N. Munyua - Jamie Sewell - Marina Showay - John Tramper - Andrew Wiggins - Erik Wilson. Additional Camera: Adrian Begon - Nat Bouman - Gretchen Cooke - Alistair Emery - Sally Low - Chris Merry - Zachary Nicholson - Rick Wagner. Camera Assistants: Eli Aronoff - Gaby Norland - Julian Pugh-Cook - Daniel Trapp - Jason Walker. Clapper Loaders: Chris Dodds - Ollie Downey - Sally Low - James Scott. —J. G.

Photographic images supplied by Karen Blessen © 2005 by Karen Blessen.
Photographic images supplied by *The Dallas Morning News* on "Kids at risk" spread © *The Dallas Morning News* and credited as follows:

David Leeson

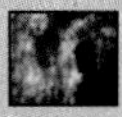
Smiley N. Pool

Erich Schlegel

Cheryl Diaz Meyer

Barbara Davidson

Michael Mulvey

From "Day of terror" spread © Gulnara Samoilova.

G. P. PUTNAM'S SONS A division of Penguin Young Readers Group. Published by The Penguin Group. Penguin Group (USA) Inc., 375 Hudson Street, New York, NY 10014, U.S.A. Penguin Group (Canada), 10 Alcorn Avenue, Toronto, Ontario, Canada M4V 3B2 (a division of Pearson Penguin Canada Inc.). Penguin Books Ltd, 80 Strand, London WC2R 0RL, England. Penguin Ireland, 25 St. Stephen's Green, Dublin 2, Ireland (a division of Penguin Books Ltd.). Penguin Group (Australia), 250 Camberwell Road, Camberwell, Victoria 3124, Australia (a division of Pearson Australia Group Pty Ltd). Penguin Books India Pvt Ltd, 11 Community Centre, Panchsheel Park, New Delhi - 110 017, India. Penguin Group (NZ), Cnr Airborne and Rosedale Roads, Albany, Auckland 1310, New Zealand (a division of Pearson New Zealand Ltd). Penguin Books (South Africa) (Pty) Ltd, 24 Sturdee Avenue, Rosebank, Johannesburg 2196, South Africa. Penguin Books Ltd, Registered Offices: 80 Strand, London WC2R 0RL, England.

 Published simultaneously in Canada. Manufactured in Hong Kong by South China Printing Co. Ltd. Design by Cecilia Yung and Gunta Alexander. Text set in Veljovic Bold. The illustrations are digital collages of pencil drawings, painted papers, newspaper headlines, and photographs. Library of Congress Cataloging-in-Publication Data Gilley, Jeremy. Peace one day / Jeremy Gilley ; illustrated by Karen Blessen. p. cm. 1. International Day of Peace—Juvenile literature. 2. Peace—Juvenile literature. 3. Gilley, Jeremy—Juvenile literature. I. Blessen, Karen, ill. II. Title. JZ5537.G55 2005 303.6'6—dc22 2004020475 ISBN 0-399-24330-5 10 9 8 7 6 5 4 3 2

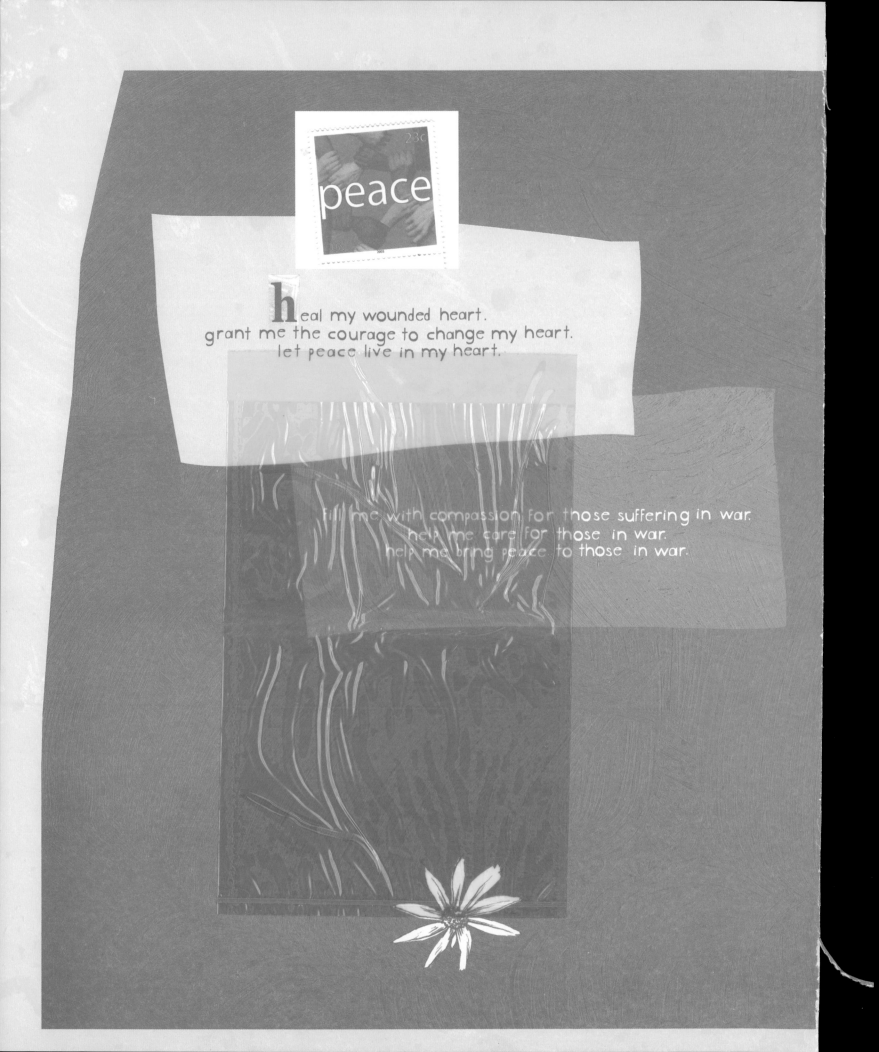

peace

heal my wounded heart.
grant me the courage to change my heart.
let peace live in my heart.

Fill me with compassion for those suffering in war.
help me care for those in war.
help me bring peace to those in war.